LITTLE BLACK DAYDREAM

AKRON SERIES IN POETRY

AKRON SERIES IN POETRY
Mary Biddinger, Editor

Steve Kistulentz, *Little Black Daydream*
Jason Bredle, *Carnival*
Emily Rosko, *Prop Rockery*
Alison Pelegrin, *Hurricane Party*
Matthew Guenette, *American Busboy*
Joshua Harmon, *Le Spleen de Poughkeepsie*
David Dodd Lee, *Orphan, Indiana*
Sarah Perrier, *Nothing Fatal*
Oliver de la Paz, *Requiem for the Orchard*
Rachel Dilworth, *The Wild Rose Asylum*
John Minczeski, *A Letter to Serafin*
John Gallaher, *Map of the Folded World*
Heather Derr-Smith, *The Bride Minaret*
William Greenway, *Everywhere at Once*
Brian Brodeur, *Other Latitudes*
Jeff Gundy, *Spoken among the Trees*
Alison Pelegrin, *Big Muddy River of Stars*
Roger Mitchell, *Half / Mask*
Ashley Capps, *Mistaking the Sea for Green Fields*
Beckian Fritz Goldberg, *The Book of Accident*
Clare Rossini, *Lingo*
Vern Rutsala, *How We Spent Our Time*
Kurt Brown, Meg Kearney, Donna Reis, Estha Weiner, eds.,
    Blues for Bill: A Tribute to William Matthews
Sharmila Voorakkara, *Fire Wheel*
Dennis Hinrichsen, *Cage of Water*
Lynn Powell, *The Zones of Paradise*

Titles published since 2003.
For a complete listing of titles published in the
series, go to www.uakron.edu/uapress/poetry

LITTLE BLACK DAYDREAM

Steve Kistulentz

The University of Akron Press
Akron, Ohio

All rights reserved • First Edition 2013 • Manufactured in the United States of America.
All inquiries and permission requests should be addressed to the Publisher, the University
of Akron Press, Akron, Ohio 44325–1703.

17   16   15   14   13   5   4   3   2   1

LIBRARY OF CONGRESS CATALOGING-IN-PUBLICATION DATA
Kistulentz, Steve.
    Little black daydream / Steve Kistulentz. — 1st ed.
        p. cm. — (Akron series in poetry)
    Poems.
    ISBN 978-1-937378-20-2 (cloth : alk. paper) —
    ISBN 978-1-937378-19-6 (pbk. : alk. paper)
    I. Title.
    PS3611.I875L58 2013
    811'.6—DC23

                        2012033425

The paper used in this publication meets the minimum requirements of ANSI/NISO
Z39.48–1992 (Permanence of Paper). ∞

Cover design: Zac Bettendorf

Little Black Daydream was designed and typeset in Centaur with Univers display by Amy
Freels and printed on sixty-pound natural and bound by BookMasters of Ashland, Ohio.

Acknowledgments

I would like to thank the editors and staff at the following journals where the original versions of these poems appeared:

"Time Grants the Two of Us Some Perspective" and "This Therapy Has Had Amazing Results" appeared in *The Antioch Review*.

"The Bungalow Club" appeared in *Barn Owl Review 4*.

"Megalography" appeared in *Barn Owl Review 5*.

"First Antiphon of Callow Youth" appeared in *Cincinnati Review*.

"Poem That Cries at the National Anthem" appeared in *580 Split*.

"Limits" appeared in *Floyd County Moonshine*.

"Using" appeared in *The Louisville Review*.

"Last of the Soviets" and "Nostalgic Love Poetry: A Poetics in Ten Parts" appeared in *The Nepotist*.

"Life During Wartime" appeared in *Puerto del Sol*.

"Procedure" and "Why I Love What Breaks Down" appeared in *Quarterly West*.

"Death Is a Hysterical Dynasty" appeared in *The Rumpus*.

"Maximalism: The Inaugural Address" appeared in *Shadowbox*.

"Maximalism: A Romance" appeared in *The Southern Review*.

"This Therapy Has Had Amazing Results" takes its title from the poem "At the Treatment Center" by Jerome Sala. The phrase "Bureau of Metropolitan Longing" in the poem "Maximalism: A Romance" is taken from a letter by Harold Brodkey. The poems that contain the word "Maximalism" in their titles do so as a tribute to late nineteenth-century political thought, which posited that the collapse of capitalism was inevitable. Advocates suggested a "maximum programme" of social-democratic policies that would replace fallen capitalism. Among the tenets of such a program are freedom, justice, and social solidarity. "Death Is a Hysterical Dynasty" is dedicated to John Hansen and Rocky LaLiberte. "Megalography" takes some of its language from a *Time* magazine column on the explosion and sinking of the Russian submarine *Kursk*, which occurred in August 2000.

I'm also thankful to the following friends for their support, guidance, and editorial assistance: Erika Meitner, Carmen Giménez-Smith, Al Maginnes, Natasha Sajé, Brian Spears.

Contents

The Symbolic Landscape of Your Childhood

... burned in the riots of '68.

A refrigerator overflowing
with the props of toy kitchens:
cornucopia of margarine,
luncheon meats,
cardboard carton of five plastic eggs.
A gallon of milk carved from birch,
painted in lead paint.
Simulacra of the land of plenty.

Talking bears. A menagerie of animals,
each with invented name and fully imagined backstory.

You fell asleep to the susurrus of what you imagined to be owls.

You used permanent marker
to draw a line on the back
of your legs,
seamed stockings,
something you'd seen in the *Midnight Mystery Movie*
with either Veronica Lake
or Lana Turner.
You were in the fifth grade.

Every summer, I passed through
your symbolic landscape,
the pick-your-own apple plantations
and woodland grottos of central Michigan,
your house so close to the highway.

Once, in the front yard, I saw a girl playing
with the corpse of a miniature dog,
making a pageant out of her vague pantomime
of resuscitation. As I drove past, she spoke,
words inaudible over the hum of tire noise
and the whip of summer wind. I imagined
this litany pouring from her lips:
Sometimes our best efforts fall slightly short.

The symbolic landscape of your childhood
is one of the few man-made objects
which can be seen from outer space,
and your town was never a town at all,
but a neighborhood, solidly working class,
Polish or Ukrainian or black Irish.
People who used to live here
drive through at irregular intervals,
shake their heads,
speak in codified slurs
like *tax base* and *property value.*
The cars parked at curbside
are no longer cars,
but burned-out carcasses.
See also *Oldsmobiles, bison, American,*
and *migratory herds.*

The first boy you ever kissed
lived in the house
I am standing in front of now.
You do not remember his name
or the cause of death.
You remember only the iridescent caftans

favored by his mother,
her perfume which smelled of vanilla.
She called you
by a string of multisyllabic nicknames,
which you also cannot remember.
The salt on your lip and charcoal in the air
and the pleasant stinging heat of a sun
warming through your shirt.
The abrasive slide of your fingers
across a popsicle stick.
A sudden urge to mow the lawn.
Benzocaine, as in the topical ointments.
See also *mercurochrome*.
Salves and medicaments.
Your grandfather: Vicks VapoRub.
The secret treasure of Sucrets,
the lasting toy you made of their tin box.

That one house where none of the children
were permitted to trick or treat, final resting place
of the symbolic landscape's first urban legend.
Apples with razor blades, or LSD, or both.

A vintage automobile on blocks
in the driveway,
the subject of your mother's nonspecific complaints.
An eyesore. Proof of said neighbor's lack of focus,
his spendthrift ways. It was an Austin Healy
or an MGB,

but in your recollection of the symbolic landscape,
the car has morphed into a 1966 GTO with redline tires,

and the driver is a boy a few years older, two tattoos.
A rosary all in silver hangs from the rear-view mirror
and an air freshener from the radio volume knob.
He puts on the *Hot Eight at Eight* and talks about
buying you new underwear, but never does.

You sit on the hood,
warmed from the radiance of the engine block,
and even in late August feel the onrushing cold
of Michigan winter, the wildness of a prairie storm
forecast in the pattern of falling leaves.
How bored you are by more rain.
The boy leaves, one arm lazing out the window,
dogs barking in reply to the squeal of tires.
A dozen house finches rattle
from their perch on the telephone wire,
and you watch as one tennis shoe hanging
there swings over your head, sliding out
an inch or two of shoelace at a time
until it drops to the asphalt below.

This is the landscape you want to see in ruins.

You have made the promise not to return
until the windows are covered
in three-quarter-inch plywood.
Perhaps you want to see it all burn.
What would it take to conjure a tornado?
Graffiti on the garage of an abandoned home says,
Fuck It All Up.

The ice cream truck starts with the trilling of its bells,
but there are no children left
to run toward the sound.

Death Is a Hysterical Dynasty

Tonight we shall read from my personal book of lamentations,
sit shiva in a room lit with those overly perfumed candles as thick
as the aluminum bat I used just last week to flip away the possum
carcass I'd found collapsed against the house. Forensics tells us
the backyard is Panama before quinine, an ecosystem
unto itself, civil war of mongoose, snake, and cat. The cause
of the possum's death was obvious, this near-biblical dryness
that lasted the summer. This morning I found a carapace,
a palmetto bug in my shower, dead in his search for water.
He got flushed, a Viking funeral; minutes later I heard about
Rocky, 48, complications from a ruptured aortic aneurysm,
who went the same week as John, 47, though by less violent means.
I'd never introduced either to my family, and now I am covering
the mirrors. Pictures from a decade ago exist without context,
the bars in them closed, marriages shattered on the pebbly coast
of installment debt, bands broken up by midnight arguments
dead men can't recall. Forgive us our trespasses, yes, but also
this literalism. Let us frame the only surviving picture of the three
of us in a rectangle of thorns before we take communion
out in the street. I will let those candles burn, burn, burn,
burn, burn to the wick, Barracuda, then tell you how
I would have laid down my life for either of those two men,
and I have nothing to offer now they have done that for me.

Using

All these kids hopped up on this dumbass vampire craze,
another fetish they'll certainly abandon after a week
of prowling the city. They will never recognize the streets
are angriest when empty, the exact hours I find myself
parked outside a house where I never lived. The morning news
is all riddles and double entendres, post-coital banter;
the weather predicts a 20 percent chance of consequences,
replays film of my worst decisions at the top of each hour.
The only things I have ever loved come in glassine packets,
and each afternoon my mailbox fills with a summons
to district court. At night the heat drives me out of the street
into a yard filled with mouse-brown bats whose sonar
has been tweaked by both the tin-tin of traffic and heavy metal
drums from the basement next door; at dawn's approach
the bats drop from the trees in little narcotic circles, half-stoned,
flying zombies singing in kittenish voice. Then the moon
disappears, and we wait to see what will rise to replace it.
Me and those bats, I mean. I pray to be led into temptation.
As a boy I learned a hymn called *O Taste and See*, so I did.

Maximalism: A Romance

At the Bureau of Metropolitan Longing, a bureaucrat dissolves
into a diffident, languorous fantasy about the idea of the boy
who sat behind her in Spanish I, but never does she dream
of the boy himself, the one she has not seen in fifteen years.
An unauthorized search of the records reveals nothing, as if even
the idea never existed. This accounts for her rheumy countenance,
the half-wince I'd mistaken for the blinding shade of cataracts.
It explains in the language of love why the supervisor is chained
to a radiator upstairs. This fallow morning, I take a number
and some Benadryl and the dreamy flush fades into a hangover's
edge and I settle in with the bums, who wait here now
that bus stations are a thing cast into the stagnant brown waters
of our racial memory. The sign above my head reads, *Now Serving*,
and instead of a number, a sideways eight, symbol of infinity.
I am not prepared for the government to speak metaphorically.
When my number is called, that same lovely clerk fixes me
with a fish-eyed stare and asks how long I have been living
in this diorama. She smiles when I say that I am a native.
When I say how I hope never to sleep again in an empty bed,
she says, *The most hopeful thing I can tell you is you are next in line.*

Postcard from a Place I Have Never Been

One condition of work-release is daily to confess
my obsessions, which I then write in disco glitter,
one gluey blossom across my permanent record.
When I eat too much of the local fruit, it gives me
clairvoyance. But I forget to write down the predictions,
instead crush cherry pits into a fine powder, chop
the powder into lines with an expired credit card.
The homeless give me quarters. Union rules require
at least one mention of the weather here. My flight
leaves on an inexact date in the nebulous future,
arrives late afternoon, two days before our first kiss.
I pay the airline $25 extra to lose my dignity between
here and Chicago. At the airport you buy it back.
When I walk to the market to buy more cherries,
a parade of kittens follows, marching in formation,
singing precise and bawdy cadence about prostitutes
and crack houses. They change the names to protect
the innocent. Signs say this mile of interstate is paved
with the bones of the great mastodons, and kept clean
by the well-meaning gentlemen of the Kiwanis Club.
Vacationers from further south sit in the lobby
watching guests from the north put on
one-act plays. On even-numbered days, only, of course.
Registered letters from the clerk of the court inform me
that it won't violate my probation to drag you across
state lines as long as I promise to return you by 8 p.m.,
mostly whole. The desk clerk is also the milkman
is the town orthodontist. Instead of leaving Bibles
at bedside, Gideons leave individual soaps printed

with couplets from the Song of Songs, or corkscrews.
I did not catch last night's plays, but promised to attend
this evening's performance. I play a slightly amplified
version of myself, with one line: *Wish you were here*.
It's a song and dance number. Everyone applauds.

Procedure

Scientific advances have now identified islands
of cellular teamwork within the human brain,
ones that trigger the spasms of unique response—
automatons punching the clock—every time
they are touched with a limited electric charge.
This is a procedure I would love to have.
Perhaps in my lifetime it will come in a do-it-yourself kit,
a bonus gift with the purchase of a bad home permanent
or a box of new razors. In front of clouded antique mirrors,
my scalp neatly peeled and unzipped, I would map my life,
saying, *Here, this is where I went insane.*
After forty-five minutes of practice,
I could induce hallucinations,
random guttural sounds, maybe even an erection,
and with my brain laid open and the safety measures defeated,
the cauterization could begin,
vaporizing any area you may have touched.

First Antiphon of Callow Youth

Profession upon the banks of Europe's greatest river,
profession upon diagnosis of the affliction. Profession
upon the receipt of unwrapped gifts and extreme unction.
A profession at the most inappropriate moment, that is to say
a profession which I must retract, amend, revise and extend.
Apprenticeship to the profession, the advantageous attachments
wherein we profess desires, our own professions so untidy
and inaccurate. How is it that at a distance of some years
you can still be the censor of my professions, and also subject,
such as it was me who made the wrong profession
at the wrong moment (I've made a profession of being wrong
this way) and it has been decades since I lost amateur status.
This profession comes from a tongue inadequate and burned,
a tongue no longer in possession of its faculties, a tongue
so ill-equipped. It is the tongue built to take the blame,
the tongue that must be contrite, the weeping tongue
that still tastes of a love neither of us dare profess.

The Bungalow Club

For the holiday, imagine my hands scraping away the dead glaze
of fifty-year-old windows, prying up loose floorboards still marked
by the rings of a brass bed where no one slept. In return I will think
of you peeling cucumbers in the exact manner of my grandmother,
making a game of it, as the long shoelaces of kelp-green skin
flutter to the bottom of the sink, leaving your whole kitchen
smelling astringent and clean. Once you are finished, the day
will give way to the temptations of gin and a dreamless sleep
I wish I could invade, if only because it's too much to think
of us in the same kitchen, the coordinated dance of cooking,
our fingers pressing greasy delights, filling each other's mouths.
It turns out that to want what I want is almost a requirement,
that middle age means learning how I once was Shiva,
all these houses I destroyed and rebuilt, a farmhouse, a condo,
now a bungalow. The foundation lists to starboard, and the sound
of home is the clatter of paws against oak and the chance
to read a new poem each night before bed, a dream I thought
as transient as the steam rising from a plate of child's pasta
in three varieties, elbows, curls, and stars. It turns out I was wrong
about all these things. I did not even know what music meant,
that song was my daughter eating, then asking for more.

A Battery-Powered Picaresque

The telegram came today: I will never reach the moon.
The directorate told us to write letters home,
break the bad news.
Later, the director himself took me into an exact mock-up
of the bedroom where I grew up, right down
to the tame pornographies pressed between mattress
and box-spring, the baggie of pot in my winter coat.
There was nothing at all symbolic about this landscape,
just a green metal desk for me to sit,
recall all the little black daydreams I'd once had.

I never was much for writing letters, immersed as I was
in metaphysics. Now the morning paper reports that metaphysics
is not what causes a spaceship to burn up on reentry;
even gravity,
which we all thought was some sure thing,
might not be what we'd hoped.

This is not that letter home.
Nor is it the righteous song
that illuminated all things,
showed the error of your ways.

Instead it is written by the five-watt glow
of a Maglite once the farmhouse
is on fire, the papers rolled and stacked
like cordwood, soaked in the sweet piss scent
of seven-dollar gasoline.
I used my last match to set it off.

Sometimes the return home requires bilateral negotiations;
complex docking maneuvers attempted, aborted,
as well as cover stories,
reservations, drink coupons,
flirty missives written from the Admiral's Club,
rejoinders that stung like Ali unleashing the overhand right.
And oh, didn't we have a fine time with our reservations?
We circled, and got hit, and circled, got hit again,
our own chorus of banter and repartee.

The saddest astronaut is not second, though.
The saddest astronaut never leaves the earth.

I want to know what victory feels like, or failing that, flight.

I want to be the sailor, swept up
in the dysphoria of V-E Day,
the one who finally got to kiss a woman
he did not know in Times Square.
The protestors could cheer us on
and shout, *The whole world is watching*,
and who knows,
maybe we'd even be as famous
as that ubiquitous photo
(admittedly Eisenstadt believed in fabricating
that which he sought to document).

I'd like to believe a kiss like that
can happen anywhere
in the tri-state area,
yet lately I am short on faith.

The bureaucrat sharpens pencils that remain sharp, unused.

The poet grinds them into inch-long stubs,
leaves them on the floor
to be mauled by well-meaning dogs.

The dogs explain in the language of dogs
how the poet has been distant lately,
a face from the faraway land
known as the sixteenth century.

The triumph of death, they say while looking over
a coffee-table book of Bruegel,
is that we still talk about it after all this...
they call it *time*.

The miracle here is that no one died.

A picaro is a roguish hero who lives by his wits.
A rascal. He talks his way out of crack houses
and shooting galleries.

He's supposed to protest, mount one last fated charge.
He consults astrologers, numismatics,
strength coaches, gastroenterologists.
The diagnosis is always the same,
one last year in the realm of the vaguely familiar.

This wanted to be the poem that told of the adventuresome squire
running his hand across the map,
repositioning his meager forces;
it wanted a strategy which suggested victory
was just one maneuver, one airlift away.

This never meant to be the poem where General Grant
gave General Lee back his sword,
told him to go home.

The love of his life was waiting there,
and it had been years since he told her
that he had been wrong
to suggest that adventure was some kind
of higher duty. It sounded foolish
to his ears, never mind what it sounded like
from his lips.

It should be clear that the antecedent for "he" is me.

As in: After one last defeat, a counter-insurgency,
he gave final orders to each of his lieutenants
in the famous words of Castro,
saying, *History will absolve me,*
and never once did he admit
that what he most wanted
was history to find him guilty.

Maximalism: Overture

O ruthless empire,
again and again in peace, I pray.

The president sports a necklace of withered human ears
during a televised appeal for more troops.
I'm told we are at war, but have yet to make the proper sacrifice.

Victors march down La Plus Belle Avenue du Monde
without the rolling snare rattle of tank battalions.
In the flowerless spring, children wave at a sky
filled with the cultish noise of drones.

Those who have fasted and those who disregarded the fast
agree on the menu for the banquet.

The secretary of consolidated debt tells his sons each morning:
When I was your age, no independent clause.
No one walks uphill to school this winter.

On the strength of a simple platform, revisionists
win a surprising victory in that fall's first elections.
Their slogan: *Help out a fellow American down on his luck.*

Soldiers at Parade Rest

The postmaster general congratulates the dead
on their excellent personal narrative, saying
they should be proud of such a definitive ending.

The rest of us watch the Giants game at the bar,
Cleveland up by seven, as if nothing has happened,
which it hasn't. The snow sifts out over the polo grounds

like a blanket over Sam Huff's memory, while the dead
parade past, each sitting on the boot of a new Cadillac,
wearing new suits from Botany 500, the dead honor guard

goose-stepping in the slow cadence of, well, the dead.
We hear rumors that someone has planned a speech.
The bartender, who looks like Y.A. Tittle, begins

bombing in five minutes. They say the children of Dresden
ran out to look at the planes and point in hopes of saving
everything. The dead are always doing nothing when it happens,

absent in their daydreams of escrow and thread counts.
We wasted everything, one said, for stainless steel appliances
and granite countertops. Our investment strategy meant

we could afford a custom tailor to measure
every grief for a toga, each wail for a wreath. The dead
dragged their left feet when marching, and when none

could march anymore, stood at parade rest, terra cotta
warriors of the PTA or the Knights of Columbus.
They hired temps for the processing, made their money

from volume, volume, volume. Each took a number,
posed for a snapshot, a thumbprint, a fitting for a new gown.
By then the rivers burned again and the black market price

for indulgences skyrocketed beyond our means. Stagflation.
I sent a care package no one was able to open
because, new law of the land, every delight must spoil and fester.

A minute before five, everyone else agreed to stand in place.

Life During Wartime

The new historians had an antipathy to fixed meanings.
Which meant no one saw the tide turning in the Middle West, blood fields
        of the republic. After the loyalist routing at Ypsilanti,
      the reconstituted government convened show trials
        broadcast
from an undisclosed location. In each of the new confederated provinces,
      the Emergency Broadcast System televised instructions on how to
      disappear.
      When we couldn't, an ambitious warden from civil defense
        suggested that the only way to live was to follow him into
        the hills;
the first-ever secretary of self-effacement spoke only in punch lines,
Wrecked him? It nearly killed him.
      Her speech at the convention—
        historians refer to it as *The Cross of Lead*—called for a new
        wave
        of pamphleteers to serve the insatiable Department of
        Pretense.
We remained indomitable, a people of unbroken spirit, so we believed
in public service messages which claimed that the laminated wood pulp
      of our desk tops could absorb the recommended daily allowance
      of millirems. The brightest among us whistled the
      prohibited music of Sousa
and Prokofiev, and hid from the wolves by immersing ourselves heel-first
      in the tide of the newer bombastic overtures such as the untitled
      piece
        colloquially referred to as *Concerto for Four Hands and*
        Breaking Plates.

They played that instead of *Hail to the Chief*.

Each Monday, an actual emergency meant an attention signal
    followed by instructions of where to tune for news and official information,
a four-minute warning, short-wave broadcasts directed at the silver
                in our molars. We removed the molars with a pair of pliers,
                Sears Craftsman, complete with comfort-cushioned grip
                        and lifetime guarantee,
    while the secretary of nostalgia explained who Sears and Roebuck used to
        be.
When the president materialized as an avuncular apparition
                in my bedroom doorway and asked me never to tell, the only way
to escape was to festoon myself with a cape fashioned from blankets
    embroidered
with cartoons of nebbishy donkeys and golden gluttonous bears.
            In the latter days of the war, at the end of hope, the cities emptied
    in their usual orderly fashion, and the secretary of civil indifference directed
        us
    to the manual for specifics on identifying potable water, lectured us
            on the protective qualities of iodine. We did not return home
            until the secretary of solid state technology said it was safe.
                We fashioned hobo bags out of surplus Che Guevara tee-
                    shirts
    and filled them with the molars of the dead. The last official broadcast
        brought news
of troops at the airport, a new government. We could no longer remember
            which republic we were supposed to be. The new minister
                of information, St. Paul, appeared in a pre-recorded
                    broadcast to warn us:
    Fallout was expected, men would be required to wear fedoras; all state
        funerals
would be accompanied by the shaken percussion of our rattling teeth.

Megalography

The only method I have not tried to reach you is telegram.
Poems are vapor, transient and marvelous and ineffective.
They remind me of those treats—first it's a candy, then it's a gum.
What other proof do you need that anything delicious is transitory?
The history of laughing on the telephone is a history of accidents.
As a child I ran a string between my bedroom and a neighbor's.
We tried to talk by using tin cans in the manner of children.
I took back both cans, held them to my eyes as binoculars.
The point was to find out just how much I could not see.
I was going to try a letter, that confluence of nostalgia and bad ideas.
A few years ago a Russian submarine exploded and sank to the bottom.
During the last ninety minutes of air, the sailors wrote letters.
We write in the dark, they said. Foolish to compare that to anything.
The title of this poem suggests we are writing about great things.
After three glasses of red wine, I sing in the imaginary voice of a sailor.
It took me years to discover all of the ordinary ways of reaching you.
We were dead when we began to speak in end-stopped proverbs.
One last prayer: let my voice be heard only after you hear my footsteps.

Maximalism: Suite Number One

Historically, the maximalists
were criticized for failure to maintain
a linear narrative or a safe following distance.
When they seized power,
the purge felt inevitable,
a tidal shift in the electorate,
but the obligatory dissident families,
Joad-like, packed up and left
the rust belt, forgot to turn out the lights.
Our nocturnal exile began in January,
the two of us playing house
in a nation-state where love was nothing
but an enriched concept
through which we explored
our hysterical realism,
headachy and self-conscious. The best
marriages, said a majority opinion,
were hand-enameled and built
on a foundation of sandstone and spite.
But that was centuries ago,
custom of another girl, another planet,
and maybe like the maximalists we felt sated,
fattened by the finger-foods of greatness.
The news prattled on, urgent commentary
about burning cities
with their burning Negro streets.
I was supposed to rage against
the plastic arts, and my monuments,
concrete glyphs on the grassy knoll,

were festooned with graffiti,
protected by Guardian Angels who stood
like a battalion of red-capped penises
surrounding a cemetery. Now our city
requires a license to panhandle,
and soon one to be heartsick;
skateboarding has always been a crime,
and the only honest trade left to ply is beggar.
We work fifty-hour weeks,
our union penance for trying
to fit all the world back into our mouths.

Maximalism: Suite Number Two

The penance for wanting every thing is to want all things.
Baptize me at the first church of invective.
I will wear a white smock blazing with the luminosity of highway paint.
My family of refugees will build a hovel from concrete jersey walls.
A roof from the cellophane from old jazz records and packs of Kool
    cigarettes.
Our table will be rich-laden.

This is reductive, the dialectic of more and more.
We will make a testimony from the preferred nuance of clarinet.
We will mark ourselves as men of wealth and taste.
We are men of taste because we prefer the nuance of clarinet to the
    blundering sax.
I make cufflinks from the molars of the dead.
I make a bespoke hair shirt from desire.

Poem That Admits Its Own Defeat

A man in a black suit delivers
an invitation printed on underpants,
one small gift in a gray felt box,
wrapped in a singular scarlet ribbon.
My date ties the ribbon 'round the base
of her throat. Someone reports in blank verse
how the bridegroom plans to crush a light bulb
under his heel, snuff his cigarettes
out in a wineglass, go back to virtuous
tradition or binge eating. He's twenty-six,
wise beyond his years. I'm obligated
to say that. Jealousy burns in me
like bituminous fuels, well, like anything
that burns, flesh eating and syphilitic,
and pathos means being non-specific.
I tell female callers how I cannot come
to the wedding because I have only
recently been diagnosed with the syndrome
of approximate answers, the fancy
medical name for wisdom. We admire
from a distance the bride's willingness
to be so public with her charity.
The Ukrainian side of the family
stuffs old pillowcases into new ones,
and the priest turns water into wine
into Canadian Club. The bride wears
black, backless and tight, a telegram
that made the groomsmen wish she'd worn it
for them, a fairy tale of sport-fucking

that never was. The band plays polkas
with burning guitar solos, and the drummer
sets his kit on fire at the end of the set.
The groom throws his shoes over the telephone
wires and places transatlantic calls
to old girlfriends, while the bride pours her father
a seventh glass of claret. We guests
adorn ourselves in Sunday best, all rented
or borrowed or woven out of the flags
of the defeated. What else is a pinstripe
suit anyway? The vows are call and response
written on back of a Topps baseball card,
and the recessional is the dance remix
of *Battle Hymn of the Republic*.
Surely this is less melodramatic
since it isn't about me, the groom's vow begins,
no antecedents expressed or implied.
The bride's mother praises the wedding portrait
as the work of a master forger,
hides it in the attic, while therapists
remain on call to help us become
the cause of our primary alienation
from our own image. The bride offers a toast,
describes marriage as an epoch once thought
to be a radical break from
the previous epoch, but it turns out to be
the same one, only with a different cast
of characters. At the appointed hour,
I begin my toast by standing on a chair;
I announce how the curvature of the earth
is no more than a gentle suggestion
like the slope of the eyeball, how to see

human history from so great a height
is to know how somewhere a child will be asked
to choose which parent dies first. My toast,
long-winded and sincere, ends with, *I surrender.*

A Military History of Seduction

We both craved full-frontal assault,
the cataclysm which generals called
a tactical error, suicidal, as they swept
the miniature tanks off the map
with the same ruler that once spanked
Catholic schoolgirls. We expected victory
by fall, not an entirely new war of thrust
and parry. I wanted strategy, to give
a little speech that began, *Patriotism requires*
our foreheads to be numbered, and in college
we read biographies of the drunk and foolhardy.
Fifty years from now, it won't be worthy
of quoting, but when I mentioned
that we have always commanded
our own doomed brigades, the scribes
took notes. I had established myself
as an expert, taught at the war college
for years. In my dress uniform,
I was luminous. My students wrote
on the dissatisfactions of youth gone wild.
Newly minted orders from headquarters
placed us on opposite sides of the restaurant,
driven out by bad music chosen by the boys
from psychological warfare. They were twenty-six,
suffused with a meager sense of history.
Lovers could no longer drink the anemic
liquors of their flamboyant past. First
I burned, and then she did, but never
once did we manage to be on fire

at the same time. At the press conference
I revealed that the prosecution of all wars
is the same: invasion, insurgency,
insurrection, counter-assault, seduction.
Torture had limited appeal, since we did it
to ourselves. Anything resembling
a tender gesture we repeated,
until the most beautiful of us
raised the white flag of surrender.

Maximalism: The Inaugural Address

I learned about the hard work of hard work from newsreels my father left around the bathroom. His little pornographies. My father the cartographer brought home the tools of his dying trade, pocket lint of model bomber wings and tank battalions; as his apprentice, I trained to place plastic brigades of soldiers in orderly rows, a blitzkrieg rolling East across a pressed paper board. In the churlish grip of adolescence, I stole my father's tools and retreated to the bunker to draw maps of islands, a few square miles of sediment and thatched huts fashioned from the whole cloth of my imagination. I turned the maps in for a grade at school, and the teacher asked what I might call these monstrosities. My answer was to call them an American project, and my answer earned me the highest marks.

We were never rich in either wealth or metaphor. Breakfast each morning was a box of government surplus cereal, ones with a send-away offer from the secretary of nostalgia, fifty box tops and $4.99 postage and handling brought instructions on how to build a homemade device to safely observe the image of the sun passing behind the moon, until the moon itself was obscured, deliberately, in a penumbra (fiery). A burning image—end times, Columbus sailing off the edge of the earth—projected onto the side wall of a milk carton festooned with reminders to call the National Center for Missing and/or Exploited Children if you had any information on the disappearance of a girl, anonymous, lost from a shopping center lot fourteen years ago, a girl who now waits to be matched with her dental records in a swampy trailer park. Then the burning image, with a counter-melody, the transient choke of chemical smoke as the girl's first-grade class photo melted through the waxed paper carton, a pinhole emergent through the burning computer-generated projection, what this girl might have looked like had she lived to be eighteen.

This burning reminds me of a holocaust of ants on concrete sidewalks, my adolescent urge to play a vengeful, Old Testament God—the wielding of a magnifying glass, through which a pinprick of light can become a weapon.

Realism has always been an associative catalog, wherein magnifying glass leads to cherry bombs purchased on a 1987 car trip to Disney World, stopping at that tourist oasis South of the Border, the most real place in the state of South Carolina, and the cherry bombs twined together into a brick-sized load that when ignited by the burning pinprick of light from a magnifying glass converted the galvanized metal of Tom Didowick's mailbox into shrapnel, a short disaster film we made of an otherwise meaningless prank. In the tiny cataclysms of that afternoon, we learn everything wrong with realism, the crushing weight of expectations.

The only gift of realism lies in its inability to explain why this milk carton device, when held at an angle of 30 degrees, produced among the arcing fires of an eclipse the face of my father, the cartographer. I recognized him from the sinuous curves of Argentina brought forth in his own hand. The ashes burned down into a smear that was maybe the same shape as the silhouette of Ohio. If you want to know what maximalism teaches, it is this: My father was a cartographer, but I never understood the truth of his work until I first learned that whatever he was compelled to draw must, at first, exist.

Last of the Soviets

So the plane never leaves Memphis, bogged down at the C gates
in a glorious caramel of bourbon and barbecue sauce. I miss
my connection for a sandwich at Neely's Interstate, return
to the Peabody Hotel where the ducks parade out of the fountain
to whisper a sincere invitation, *Join us for a rooftop nightcap,*
meaning don't bother hurtling across Shelby County's darkest
corners just to return to the life you've spent a sodden weekend
railing against. This is not the first time birds have spoken to me.

I am not being figurative at all. At the top of the moonscape dunes
of Kill Devil Hills, I watched a flying V of Canada geese carve
and flutter among children's cartoonish kites, as if the last
of the Soviets had jammed their radar. They asked for direction
so I pointed them south, and as for me, once they heard my story,
they gave direction too, saying, *You'll be sorry,* and *It will end in tears.*

Poem That Cries at the National Anthem

The first act of the national assembly:
proclamation of a new anthem,
We Almost Lost Detroit.

Also, a reconstitution of the rituals of High Mass,
beginning with the resurrection
of the ancient language
no one speaks.

So ordered.

This is one way, these distractions, to hide your crimes.

The priest said the empty seats reminded him
of Municipal Stadium, the mistake by the lake.

The mistake by the lake reminded me of a girl.

The Archbishop of Hamtramck took his scepter
and taught the Boy Scouts
how to step
to the new music,
and we would have had a parade, too,
except no one had decided yet
on the new flag,
and music was still the atonal dirge,
the rattling teeth
that woke us each night.

Still this was no day for work.

I volunteered at the hospital,
reading the day's headlines
to the veterans.
I passed around pens
for them to annotate the paper.

The newspaper was from November 1973.

They scratched out the names in each news story
to write in their own,
because it is so much easier to believe
in crimes committed by someone
with a familiar name.
The one with the red marker wrote,
Redacted for national security purposes,
across his hospital chart, his bracelet,
his forehead.

Tell us again about Vietnam, another said,
the same voice that used to ask
about the hundred-acre wood.

They gathered in a circle   .
and set fire to the cafeteria tables,
demanded, *Tell us again about the assassinations.*

I followed my directions completely,
so I did no harm
to wheat, wine, or oil.

The baseball game was entirely my mistake.

I should have expected the gesture.
Veterans. The holiday. Hot dogs and six-dollar beer,
the vendor's sideways look
at the guy who asked for ketchup.

No one talked about bombs bursting in air.
No one talked either about
the dawn's early light,
which to them was fireglow,
future visions of the corporate wars,
the cadmium red and candy apple gray
that told us fallout was expected.

Instead the veterans chose up sides,
asked to be driven to the old stadium.
They held a séance to conjure the ghost
of Dave Righetti,
who once threw a no-hitter
on the Fourth of July.

Not until the first player stepped
into the batter's box
did we remember
that we were supposed to sing.

Nostalgic Love Poetry: A Poetics in Ten Parts

1.   Any discussion of the past must include
passing mention of the phases of the moon,
which must always be waning.

2.   Memory should be more than the pornography
of uncensored short films, since whatever
remembrance you conjure must leave room for my rebuttal.

3.   You must put me in these poems as well,
for I was never as pretty as I was then,
resplendent in long hair and pink shirts (plural),
whereas now I am nothing but an eavesdropper
who steals kiss after kiss in bathrooms
and on patios up and down the eastern seaboard.

4 (a).   If I am to be caught while I kiss your neck, we should lie.
I will pretend not to notice how your neck stiffens
but your body yields, and I will wait for you to say
whatever you must say, a placeholder, to absolve yourself.

4 (b).   Having ██████████████
████████████████████████ (redacted).

4 (c).   Yes, let's.

5.   This is nostalgia, remember, and the film
was called *The Way We Were*, past tense.

6.   Someone should figure out how to bottle this smell,
an alchemy as mysterious as splitting the atom ...
(excerpt) ... We spray this perfume over
our pillows to induce dreams of unattainable things.

7. We believe in the disease model of nostalgia
    and our powerlessness over it.

8. If we are lucky, we are allowed to forget enough
    of these rules before we write them down,
    where they become our weakest effort
    to date at making amends.

9. Under this waning moon you should recall
    the one perfume that you have never forgotten,
    hold its fragrance deep in your nose like a bloodhound
    chasing Cool Hand Luke and break down that smell
    into its constituent elements—honey, orange, vermillion,
    sweat, marshland, chocolate frosting, wet leather,
    wet everything, plastic, latex, the dry gag of baby powder
    that puffed out in small smokeless clouds
    from the old-style condoms no one remembered to use.

A Psalm for Billy Sathmary,
Loneliest Child in the Seventh Grade

November 27, 1966–January 25, 2001

Forgive me this venial sin, not recognizing your ghost
when it sidled past my office during last November's rains,
trailing a slender yet elegant beam of longing and melancholy
like Pigpen's cloud. I followed this shade, your shade,
like one of the great ships of yesterday sliding the larded rails
down to the sea, never to return to the place it was born.
So then I began to see you everywhere, fleeing as a bird
does to its mountain: a reformer tormented by sons
of party officials; turtlenecked and cowering in a coffeehouse
corner; the orphaned rogue around the schoolyard's periphery,
not one righteous fist ready to break the teeth of the wicked
in your defense. Then you emerged in the cheap-seat clouds
of El Greco's *The Dormition*, not as obvious as Christ
the Pantocrator or a lesser saint, just an amorphous cherub,
gelatinous and gender-confused, cheerleader for the apocalypse.
I truly began to worry once you appeared in a photograph
by Diane Arbus, *Jewish Giant at Home with His Parents
in the Bronx, NY, 1970*, because to see this photo
is to know how easily life's margins are defined.
The giant's name was Eddie Carmel, and he died
at the age of thirty-six of a glandular disorder his parents
could not even pronounce. The Carmels, a handsome
pair, average height, God-fearing, stared at Eddie
and his monstrous body the way we must have stared
at you, Billy, and as their son bent in half to avoid
hitting his head on the glass tulips of the chandelier
or on the oaken frame of the doorway, all of us unindicted
co-conspirators from seventh grade began to ask the same

rhetorical question, *How did we fail to notice the monster
in our midst, an eight-foot golem as large as the davenport?*

I suspect your last words were, *Uncle,* or *Please don't,*
the last thing I can remember hearing you speak,
a litany I now hear as your prayer. Forgive me, too,
that I cannot portray you as more than the gawky fat kid,
standard issue in every seventh-grade class, old soul
in an old man's white belt, a black lunch pail stuffed
with lunches fit for us proles: deviled ham on Wonder bread,
the buried treasures of Pop Rocks, Zots, Bottle Caps,
Razzles, Gold Rush bubble gum, a family-sized bag
of potato chips some twenty years before we thought
to fear partially hydrogenated oils. Yes, I know how
a tale of regret becomes familiar, the sorrows of young Billy
as evinced by a convincing disinterest in kickball and girls,
the sausage-casing fingers that could never follow
the body's simplest operating instructions. At the recital,
you pantomimed *Nadia's Theme,* a song the orchestra knew
colloquially as the music to *The Young and the Restless,*
because your fingers could not speak the foreign language
of pizzicato on a violin cut down to student scale.

Forgive me also for that summer's make-out parties
especially when Michelle C. freshened her lip gloss
to kiss every one of us, but drew the line at fat Billy.
Absolve me of my guilt for making such a tepid effort
here, on this page. Instead remember me, O dead friend,
when you shall come into your kingdom, and if not,
grant me only a pitiless blessing, the right to remember
you as a martyr, as I can think of no one else who might
know how prayers, if never fulfilled, must at least be heard.

Those of us who believe in retribution, karma,
or even the Old Testament type of vengeance
foresworn by the New Covenant understand
why it has become customary punishment for me
to see you in every awkward child I meet. Forgive, too,
my denials, because I hate what you remind me of,
how you indict me even from your grave. I wish
you could hear what I've learned from your example:
The richness of life's blessings comes only to those
who keep the skin of an elephant, the heart of a child.
All this recollection is the work of my own wicked hands,
and I have changed my mind. Keep on haunting me.

Haunt me because I have sinned without number.
If I am hungry, toss me scraps which I will wash down
with flagons of vinegar until you understand: We forsook you
only because we saw you as rich. Haunt me
by filling my dreams with luscious banquets, a table
with a bounteous lack of nothing, and force me to watch
as you eat all of the world you can stomach.

Limits

These persistent equations have been troubling me:
If a rocket leaves Pyongyang at an initial velocity of a
thousand feet per second,
how many survivors wander Portland's burning streets by noon? A number
that approaches, but does not equal, zero. Can you see how calculus
failed us here? In the assassination attempts, we approached our leaders
asymptotically.

Limits arose organically from both form and event,
yet they could also be articulated by the use of a mutually
agreed upon safeword.
In the event of an actual emergency the limit of negative one remains one,
which Avogadro trademarked as the loneliest number. Last fall
I unsuccessfully petitioned the Union of Concerned Poets to
reclassify this number
as the poetic constant. Or to name Avogadro,
posthumously,
our next bartender laureate.

My research has revealed the only possible
explanation
for his foresight is loneliness, the spirit
approaching absolute zero, the crippling
self-doubt he must have felt, calculating the molecular weight of
Chianti,
of whisky and water in solution, a first step in his seminal work to establish
the saturation point of the human heart. When we speak of
entities such as the heart, isn't it a mistake to attempt to
count lovers, to compile

totals as if we are eye-shaded and Dickensian in our rampant cynicism?

This is the very problem which tormented Avogadro's later work,
his inability to distinguish alternate states of the heart. He died
without ever testing the antithesis: a thing can be both
constant and variable.
Better to remain constant and approach truth at a discrete angle.

For those of us not well-versed in the physical sciences, a quick translation
suggests
that while we can veer as close as possible to certainty, we must resign ourselves
to the limits of language. Hidden in Avogadro's equation is this note:
The absolute value of truth shares the same spiritual weight
as liquid nitrogen and is equally hazardous to the cravings of our
longing touch.

This Therapy Has Had Amazing Results

A treatment protocol:
insomnia,
reading between the lines with magnifiers,
wine of an unpronounceable chateau,
Sea Island cotton shirts, four hundred threads to the inch,
iced tea on a brick patio,
pâté de campagne and a table in the window to flaunt you,
stargazers and Easter lilies in place of the common rose,
films where I have memorized the dialogue,
ah, one of these days, Miss Golightly,
cassettes that begin and end
with Leonard Cohen rumbling about God and love,
essays in favor of the sensitive man,
dressing you in a thrift shop,
a shooting jacket and a Girl Scout miniskirt,
black currant tea, sickly sweet,
velvet, velour, silk, and latex,
wax, scissors, tin foil, and perfume,
razors, a new suit, and cologne,
the artist as madman:
That is a given;
we saw it in a museum.
Well, this therapy of yours
has had amazing results.

Why I Love What Breaks Down

for Dave Smith

I've broken most things a man can and survived,
though I move with the rigid steps of some older man
who is not me; a few scars I can show off,
a few I cannot, though I claim to love them all
the same. A purple heart for the starburst
on the bony knob of my ankle where bone
and ligament saw air for the first time.
What in this world isn't a narrative
where every fracture tells a story? We all keep
a childhood fondness for picking scabs;
that's why, after eating the cooling asphalt
of a rain glassy road, I fixed that bike
instead of selling it for scrap. There's a Royal
portable typewriter behind me, on the rotten sill
of a window with cracked panes, dried out caulk.
I'll get around to fixing all of it soon,
and that could be why I love what breaks down,
because it gives me something to do.
Part of being human is to specialize in repair,
and pray that when called upon, you are able
to raise the hood of a rusted Chevrolet,
see frayed belts thrown about the machine,
and know the difference between what is broken,
what can be fixed, and what was never worth the trouble.

Poem That Wishes It Could Touch Your Face

Overnight activity in Battle Creek, longhand messages coded
by Hello Kitty flashlight, the disordered world wherein again
we are forever twelve or thirteen, chewing the wrong flavored gum.
Mystery meant Michelle C., the face that launched a thousand
penis jokes, the girl who slathered her lips in grape gloss
to practice-kiss us at the bus stop, even other girls. I knew
our first kiss would be perfect, if only I could bite the inside
of my own mouth first, be consumptive, wracked with guilt,
render unto her mouth the venom of otherworldly solitude.
For the science fair, her project was a little boxed assemblage
of the bus stop on Macomb Street, wherein one girl—raven-
haired of course—held a box on her hip, a dozen boys waiting
for the favor of her saccharine kiss. You have seen the girl
among the survivors at the Art Institute. She wore patent
Mary Janes, tee-shirts that read, *Not to be removed under penalty of law.*
I wanted not only a kiss but a mind-meld; she wanted someone
to call her *hot*, an unbalanced equation. The girls I wanted
were cave drawings, inscrutable, just as the boys who waited
to kiss Michelle were busy fools, hands in pockets. I waited
twenty-seven years for that bus, and now I am a traveler
who does not speak the language and rarely rides.
How I wanted her to marvel at my argument, forsake others,
cleave to me in the ceremonial parade of the couples skate.
This is the part that wishes I could skate. Until today
there had been nothing lovelier than a girl waiting for a bus
who smoked a Virginia Slim stolen from her mother's purse,
whose mouth burned of natural and artificial flavors.
This is where I tell you I've since cracked the code.
Recent intelligence suggests a counter-offensive; recruits

are refusing to cross the many rivers between us. They say
you are in Lincoln Park, holed up in an insurgent stronghold.
I tell them I am willing to be first over the walls,
that the orders given by doomed and foolhardy generals
always begin with the same words: *I know what I'm doing.*

Time Grants the Two of Us Some Perspective

The orders once we returned home were simple:
Burn the past, you said.
So I did,
clear cutting my way through
anything sentimental,
trying to maintain an economy of words,
describing my passion the way it is—
succinct, direct, threatening.
But you were right when you told me
these poems needed length,
depth of feeling.
There should be a balance,
since the cool tone of my words is strength.
Except you meant cool as in *distant*.
The metaphors spoke like Gospels.
That bit about my heart—
how it lives as two tectonic plates—
was right on.
But how do I say the rest of it?
A mountain preacher handling snakes
has always been foolish,
and you disregarded orders,
kept every foolish thing
I wrote.
I would keep the letters
folded in a Bible,
and hope that *Thou Shalt Not* could evolve
into something lenient,
contemporary.

The pictures you must keep
at your office,
undisturbed in the bottom drawer.
Maybe in time, I will write the rest of it
down, in paragraphs instead of stanzas,
since I doubt we will produce
a noteworthy correspondence,
or together become famous,
envied by the sympathetics;
if anything, now that I am finished,
no one will know,
except a wronged spouse,
since I so rarely show these poems to anyone,
and it is my fervent prayer
you did not keep a diary.

Portrait of You at the Victory Banquet

The press argued for weeks over the right name for it,
surrender, victory, or merely the triumph of the inevitable.
Former rebels bussed plates, scrubbed bathrooms,
whistled Sousa marches as they ground the drinking glasses
into a fine powder and shook slivers into the bread dough,
which contained a centuries-old starter culture. One guy
came by the table and said the two of us were a moment
history must record, like Mussolini ripping open his shirt,
defying the guards to shoot him square in the chest.
Then he asked to paint our portrait in oil for a tank
of gas or a ride to Kalamazoo. You covered your face
like a troubled starlet, shooed him away. The main course,
fatted calf roasted with garlic and rosemary, came with
the coveted mouth feel of victory, and we applauded the chef
who thanked us for returning to the scene of our folly.
We drank wine from the bodega, beer from the gas station.
We found a hospital vending machine and pressed
the button for coffee light with one sugar, but the cup
tilted to the side and overflowed. We never got our quarters
back. The broadcasts resumed during dessert, instructions
on where to tune in the event of actual sexual tension.
Dessert itself was Jell-O, its red color staining your mouth
so its corners raised into a clown-like curve. I did not
let you wipe your lips. Afterwards, we drove down
into the city center past the tool and die and the plant
where percussion once meant the stamping of rolled steel
into tailfin fenders, and you said, *We are driving through
the symbolic landscape of my childhood*, as if naming it
caused the burning houses to appear on all sides. I found

a parking space in front of an abandoned Georgian mansion
(what hadn't been abandoned by then?) across from
the abandoned Unitarian Church around the corner from
the abandoned bowling alley. We walked to a boxwood maze
that had grown wild, untethered, got ourselves lost
near a series of fountains. You said if this were a French movie
you'd throw yourself in, but it wasn't French. It was a war
story or a disaster film or a speculative vision of America
without oceans. *Disaster film, definitely,* said the guy
who wanted to paint us, and he couldn't figure out how
to make the camera rotate around us as we kissed.
There wasn't even a beach. We took out a notebook
to catalog the who and what that had survived,
the buildings with rusted windows where we huddled
by the fire of a butane torch. Children here built crafts
out of abandoned hypodermics, and the city sold us a house
for a dollar once we promised never to leave. Your hair
was brilliantine and perfect, gleaming like a muscle car
Simonized to shine its brightest on the repetitive loops
of a Friday night, 1966, before the city had even burned once.
At a clearing we came to a stone pedestal for an abandoned
statue, and we climbed, watched the food carts go strolling out
past the rusted city buses. You raised your eyes to the horizon,
that afflicted look so familiar in our great leaders, told me
you were high up, enough so that you could only see the past.
I chiseled your name in the base of blue granite, put the date
of your death as a very long time in the amorphous future.
A marching band showed up—old uniforms moth-eaten, the brass
with lips too weak to play—so they hummed songs for us,
and we called it an unveiling. I took my place behind you, asked
that you raise one foot off the ground, the universal language
which meant you had been wounded in battle, but survived.

About the Author

Steve Kistulentz is the author of two books of poetry. The first, *The Luckless Age*, was selected by Nick Flynn as the winner of the Benjamin Saltman Award. He holds an MFA from the Iowa Writer's Workshop and a doctorate from Florida State University, where he held the Edward and Marie Kingsbury Fellowship for Excellence in Thought. He lives in Jackson, Mississippi, and teaches English and creative writing at Millsaps College. Poems from *Little Black Daydream* have appeared in *Barn Owl Review*, *The Cincinnati Review*, *The Louisville Review*, *The Southern Review*, and elsewhere.